~ POETRY FOR KIDS ~

Walt Whitman

~ POETRY FOR KIDS ~
Walt Whitman

EDITED BY
KAREN KARBIENER, PhD

ILLUSTRATED BY KATE EVANS

MoonDance

Inspiring | Educating | Creating | Entertaining

© 2017 Quarto Publishing Group USA Inc.

First Published in 2017 by MoonDance Press, an imprint of The Quarto Group.
6 Orchard Road, Suite 100, Lake Forest, CA 92630, USA.
T (949) 380-7510 **F** (949) 380-7575 **www.QuartoKnows.com**

MoonDance Press titles are also available at discount for retail, wholesale, promotional, and bulk purchase. For details, contact the Special Sales Manager by email at specialsales@quarto.com or by mail at The Quarto Group, Attn: Special Sales Manager, 401 Second Avenue North, Suite 310, Minneapolis, MN 55401 USA.

ISBN: 978-1-63322-150-5

Original text © 2017 Karen Karbiener
Illustrations © 2017 Kate Evans

Cover and interior design: Melissa Gerber

Printed in China
3 5 7 9 10 8 6 4

Contents

INTRODUCTION, 6

WALT'S WELCOME, 7

Song of the Open Road (excerpt), 7

STARTING FROM PAUMANOK, 8

There Was a Child Went Forth (two excerpts), 8
Paumanok, 10
The Sleepers (excerpt), 11
Out of the Cradle Endlessly Rocking (two excerpts), 12
Beginning My Studies, 13
When I Heard the Learn'd Astronomer, 13
Crossing Brooklyn Ferry (three excerpts), 14
A Font of Type, 16

WALT WHITMAN, A KOSMOS, OF MANHATTAN THE SON, 17

Walt Whitman's Caution, 17
I Sing the Body Electric (excerpt), 18
A Woman Waits for Me (excerpt), 20
City of Ships (excerpt), 21
Give Me the Splendid Silent Sun, 22
Song of Myself (six excerpts), 24
Shut Not Your Doors, 30
Calamus 9, 31

THE WOUND-DRESSER, 32

Beat! Beat! Drums!, 32
The Wound-Dresser (excerpt), 33
Come Up From the Fields Father, 34
As Toilsome I Wander'd Virginia's Woods, 36
O Captain! My Captain!, 37
Aboard at a Ship's Helm, 38

THE GOOD GRAY POET, 39

O Me! O Life!, 39
On the Beach at Night, 40
A Noiseless Patient Spider, 42
Thanks in Old Age, 43
Poets to Come, 44

WHAT WALT WAS THINKING, 45

INDEX, 48

Introduction

Listener up there! Here you.... what have you to confide to me?
Look in my face while I snuff the sidle of evening,
Talk honestly, for no one else hears you, and I stay only a minute longer.

Walt Whitman wants to speak with you—yes, you! What's more, he wants to listen to you too. "How can a book communicate so directly with me?" you might wonder as you wander through the freely flowing poems of *Leaves of Grass.* "This is no book," Walt answers from another page. "Who touches this touches a man."

Walt started a revolution in American cultural history by breaking all the rules. He got personal with his readers instead of maintaining a "safe" distance across the pages. He liberated poetry from traditional rhyme and meter, writing in long lines that sound—and even look—natural and free. He celebrated people and experiences that weren't considered proper subjects for literature, and preached equality across gender, race, and class. And he believed in poetry's power to change the world.

Walt is now recognized as America's greatest poet, and his collection of poetry entitled *Leaves of Grass* is considered America's cultural Declaration of Independence, second only to our political Declaration of 1776. But in many ways he is the least likely candidate for this title and honor. The story of Walt's journey as an artist is just about as exciting as his work, so the poems in this book have been carefully selected to guide you through his unconventional and extraordinary career.

This book's first section, "Starting From Paumanok," includes poems that focus on Walt's earliest years and his development as a poet. You will meet him on the beaches of his beloved "Paumanok" (the Algonquin tribe's name for Long Island), be there when he learns his poetic gift was inspired by nature, not school ("Out of the Cradle Endlessly Rocking"), and travel with him to Brooklyn, where he discovered his deep love for humanity ("Crossing Brooklyn Ferry").

"Walt Whitman, a Kosmos, of Manhattan the Son" is named after one of the most famous lines in "Song of Myself," Walt's great personal epic. These selections were written in his artistic prime, when he proclaimed himself and his work an independent universe or "kosmos." At the center of it all for Walt was New York City, and these poems reflect its influence.

The section entitled "The Wound-Dresser" includes Walt's greatest Civil War poems. In the title poem and other selections, you'll find that he wasn't just an onlooker or commentator on the war, but volunteered countless hours as a nurse and letter-writer for wounded soldiers.

"The Good Gray Poet" was a popular nickname for Walt in his later years. These poems present a man who has gained much in his life, including fearlessness of death. Though he did not receive the recognition he wanted, he welcomes you to fulfill his promise: "Leaving it to you to prove and define it,/ Expecting the main things from you" ("Poets to Come").

Walt and I both hope that, as you "listeners" look down into this book's "face," you'll find messages just for you. And as Whitman's life and work are revealed on the following pages, perhaps you'll be compelled to respond to him as so many others have. You may just find that you, too, have poetry inside of you.

Walt's Welcome

Song of the Open Road (excerpt)

Camerado, I give you my hand!
I give you my love more precious than money,
I give you myself before preaching or law;
Will you give me yourself? Will you come travel with me?
Shall we stick by each other as long as we live?

Camerado: Walt's own term for a true and loyal friend, probably influenced by the term "camaraderie" (mutual trust and friendship) or "camarade" (a French word for friend)

Starting From Paumanok

There Was A Child Went Forth (two excerpts)

There was a child went forth every day,
And the first object he looked upon and received with wonder or pity or love or dread, that object
    he became,
And that object became part of him for the day or a certain part of the day . . . . or
    for many years or stretching cycles of years.

The early lilacs became part of this child,
And grass, and white and red morningglories, and white and red clover, and the song of the
    phoebe-bird,
And the March-born lambs, and the sow's pink-faint litter, and the mare's foal, and
    the cow's calf, and the noisy brood of the barnyard or by the mire of the pond-
    side . . and the fish suspending themselves so curiously below there . . and the
    beautiful curious liquid . . and the water-plants with their graceful flat heads . . .

These became part of that child who went forth every day, and who now goes and
    will always go forth every day,
And these become of him or her that peruses them now.

Mire: swampy ground
Peruses: observes

8

Paumanok

Sea-beauty! stretch'd and basking!
One side thy inland ocean laving, broad, with copious commerce, steamers, sails,
And one the Atlantic's wind caressing, fierce or gentle—mighty hulls dark-gliding in the
    distance.
Isle of sweet brooks of drinking-water—healthy air and soil!
Isle of the salty shore and breeze and brine!

Laving: flowing
Copious: abundant
Brine: salty water

The Sleepers (excerpt)

Now I tell what my mother told me today as we sat at dinner together,
Of when she was a nearly grown girl living home with her parents on the old homestead.

A red squaw came one breakfasttime to the old homestead,
On her back she carried a bundle of rushes for rushbottoming chairs;
Her hair straight shiny coarse black and profuse halfenveloped her face,
Her step was free and elastic . . . . her voice sounded exquisitely as she spoke.
My mother looked in delight and amazement at the stranger,
She looked at the beauty of her tallborne face and full and pliant limbs,
The more she looked upon her she loved her,
Never before had she seen such wonderful beauty and purity;
She made her sit on a bench by the jamb of the fireplace . . . . she cooked food for her,
She had no work to give her but she gave her remembrance and fondness.

The red squaw staid all the forenoon, and toward the middle of the afternoon she went away;
O my mother was loth to have her go away,
All the week she thought of her . . . . she watched for her many a month,
She remembered her many a winter and many a summer,
But the red squaw never came nor was heard of there again.

Squaw: a Native American woman
Rushbottoming: having a seat made with long grasses
Exquisitely: in a very fine and beautiful manner
Tallborne: Walt's word for "long," with a feeling of nobility borrowed from the word "highborn"
Jamb: side post

11

Out of the Cradle Endlessly Rocking (two excerpts)

Once, Paumanok,
When the snows had melted, and the Fifth Month grass was growing,
Up this sea-shore, in some briers,
Two guests from Alabama—two together,
And their nest, and four light-green eggs, spotted with brown,
And every day the he-bird, to and fro, near at hand,
And every day the she-bird, crouched on her nest, silent, with bright eyes,
And every day I, a curious boy, never too close, never disturbing them,
Cautiously peering, absorbing, translating.

Shine! Shine!
Pour down your warmth, great Sun!
While we bask—we two together.

Two together!
Winds blow South, or winds blow North,
Day come white, or night come black,
Home, or rivers and mountains from home,
Singing all time, minding no time,
If we two but keep together.

Bird! (then said the boy's Soul,)
Is it indeed toward your mate you sing? or is it mostly to me?
For I that was a child, my tongue's use sleeping,
Now that I have heard you,
Now in a moment I know what I am for—I awake,
And already a thousand singers—a thousand songs, clearer, louder, more sorrowful than yours,
A thousand warbling echoes have started to life within me,
Never to die.

Fifth Month: the Quaker version of the month of May
Briers: prickly plants

Beginning My Studies

Beginning my studies the first step pleas'd me so much,
The mere fact consciousness, these forms, the power of motion,
The least insect or animal, the senses, eyesight, love,
The first step I say awed me and pleas'd me so much,
I have hardly gone and hardly wish'd to go any farther,
But stop and loiter all the time to sing it in ecstatic songs.

Loiter: linger
Ecstatic: full of joy

When I Heard the Learn'd Astronomer

When I heard the learn'd astronomer;
When the proofs, the figures, were ranged in columns before me;
When I was shown the charts and the diagrams, to add, divide, and measure them;
When I, sitting, heard the astronomer, where he lectured with much applause in the lecture-room,
How soon, unaccountable, I became tired and sick;
Till rising and gliding out, I wander'd off by myself,
In the mystical moist night-air, and from time to time,
Look'd up in perfect silence at the stars.

Unaccountable: without an explanation

Crossing Brooklyn Ferry (three excerpts)

Flood-tide below me! I see you face to face!
Clouds of the west—sun there half an hour high—I see you also face to face.
Crowds of men and women attired in the usual costumes, how curious you are to me!
On the ferry-boats the hundreds and hundreds that cross, returning home, are more curious to me
    than you suppose,
And you that shall cross from shore to shore years hence are more to me, and more in my
    meditations, than you might suppose.

It avails not, time nor place—distance avails not,
I am with you, you men and women of a generation, or ever so many generations hence,
Just as you feel when you look on the river and sky, so I felt,
Just as any of you is one of a living crowd, I was one of a crowd,
Just as you are refresh'd by the gladness of the river and the bright flow, I was refresh'd,
Just as you stand and lean on the rail, yet hurry with the swift current, I stood yet was hurried,
Just as you look on the numberless masts of ships and the thick-stemm'd pipes of steamboats, I
    look'd.

What is it then between us?
What is the count of the scores or hundreds of years between us?

Whatever it is, it avails not—distance avails not, and place avails not,
I too lived, Brooklyn of ample hills was mine,
I too walk'd the streets of Manhattan island, and bathed in the waters around it,
I too felt the curious abrupt questionings stir within me,
In the day among crowds of people sometimes they came upon me,
In my walks home late at night or as I lay in my bed they came upon me.

Hence: in the future
Avails: helps or benefits

15

A Font of Type

This latent mine—these unlaunch'd voices—passionate powers,
Wrath, argument, or praise, or comic leer, or prayer devout,
(Not nonpareil, brevier, bourgeois, long primer merely,)
These ocean waves arousable to fury and to death,
Or sooth'd to ease and sheeny sun and sleep,
Within the pallid slivers slumbering.

Latent: hidden
Unlaunch'd: not yet set free
Leer: glance
Nonpareil, brevier, bourgeois, long primer: sizes
  of type, from smallest to largest
Pallid: pale-colored, like a sheet of paper (Whitman's "slivers")

Walt Whitman, a Kosmos, of Manhattan the Son

Walt Whitman's Caution

To The States, or any one of them, or any city of The States, *Resist much, obey little*;
Once unquestioning obedience, once fully enslaved;
Once fully enslaved, no nation, state, city, of this earth, ever afterward resumes its liberty.

I Sing the Body Electric (excerpt)

A man's body at auction!
I help the auctioneer—the sloven does not half know his business.

Gentlemen, look on this wonder!
Whatever the bids of the bidders, they cannot be high enough for it,
For it the globe lay preparing quintillions of years, without one animal or plant,
For it the revolving cycles truly and steadily rolled.

In this head the all-baffling brain,
In it and below it the making of the attributes of heroes.

Examine these limbs, red, black, or white—they are so cunning in tendon and nerve,
They shall be stript that you may see them.

Exquisite senses, life-lit eyes, pluck, volition,
Flakes of breast-muscle, pliant back-bone and neck, flesh not flabby, good-sized arms and legs,
And wonders within there yet.

Within there runs blood—the same old blood! the same red running blood!
There swells and jets a heart—there all passions, desires, reachings, aspirations,
Do you think they are not there because they are not expressed in parlors and lecture-rooms?

This is not only one man—this is the father of those who shall be fathers in their turns,
In him the start of populous states and rich republics,
Of him countless immortal lives, with countless embodiments and enjoyments.

How do you know who shall come from the offspring of his offspring through the centuries?
Who might you find you have come from yourself, if you could trace back through the centuries?

Sloven: careless, vulgar person
All-baffling: Walt's word for "mystifying everyone"
Pluck: spirited courage
Volition: the power to make one's own choices

A Woman Waits for Me (excerpt)

They are not one jot less than I am,
They are tann'd in the face by shining suns and blowing winds,
Their flesh has the old divine suppleness and strength,
They know how to swim, row, ride, wrestle, shoot, run, strike, retreat, advance, resist, defend themselves,
They are ultimate in their own right—they are calm, clear, well-possess'd of themselves.

Jot: bit (Walt is thinking of tiny drips from his pen)
Suppleness: flexibility

City of Ships (excerpt)

City of the world! (for all races are here;
All the lands of the earth make contributions here;)
City of the sea! city of hurried and glittering tides!
City whose gleeful tides continually rush or recede, whirling in and out, with eddies and foam!
City of wharves and stores! city of tall façades of marble and iron!
Proud and passionate city! mettlesome, mad, extravagant city!

Eddies: currents of water
Façades: building fronts
Mettlesome: spirited
Mad: crazy

Give Me the Splendid Silent Sun

1.

Give me the splendid silent sun, with all his beams full-dazzling;

Give me juicy autumnal fruit, ripe and red from the orchard;

Give me a field where the unmow'd grass grows;

Give me an arbor, give me the trellis'd grape;

Give me fresh corn and wheat—give me serene-moving animals, teaching content;

Give me nights perfectly quiet, as on high plateaus west of the Mississippi, and I looking up at the stars;

Give me odorous at sunrise a garden of beautiful flowers, where I can walk undisturb'd;

Give me for marriage a sweet-breath'd woman, of whom I should never tire;

Give me a perfect child—give me, away, aside from the noise of the world, a rural domestic life;

Give me to warble spontaneous songs, reliev'd, recluse by myself, for my own ears only;

Give me solitude—give me Nature—give me again,

O Nature, your primal sanities!

—These, demanding to have them, (tired with ceaseless excitement, and rack'd by the war-strife;)

These to procure, incessantly asking, rising in cries from my heart,

While yet incessantly asking, still I adhere to my city;

Day upon day, and year upon year, O city, walking your streets,

Where you hold me enchain'd a certain time, refusing to give me up;

Yet giving to make me glutted, enrich'd of soul—you give me forever faces;

(O I see what I sought to escape, confronting, reversing my cries;

I see my own soul trampling down what it ask'd for.)

Recluse: alone
Primal sanities: basic sources of
  contentment and joy
Procure: find
Incessantly: constantly
Glutted: overfull
Phantoms incessant: constant parade
  of spirits
Troittoirs: sidewalks
Interminable: endless
Wharves: docks
Repletion: overfullness
Brigade: large body of army troops

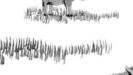

2.

Keep your splendid silent sun;

Keep your woods, O Nature, and the quiet places by the woods;

Keep your fields of clover and timothy, and your cornfields and orchards;

Keep the blossoming buckwheat fields, where the Ninth-month bees hum;

Give me faces and streets! give me these phantoms incessant and endless along the trottoirs!

Give me interminable eyes! give me women! give me comrades and lovers by the thousand!

Let me see new ones every day! let me hold new ones by the hand every day!

Give me such shows! give me the streets of Manhattan!

Give me Broadway, with the soldiers marching—give me the sound of the trumpets and drums!

(The soldiers in companies or regiments—some, starting away, flush'd and reckless;

Some, their time up, returning, with thinn'd ranks—young, yet very old, worn, marching, noticing nothing;)

—Give me the shores and the wharves heavy-fringed with the black ships!

O such for me! O an intense life! O full to repletion, and varied!

The life of the theatre, bar-room, huge hotel, for me!

The saloon of the steamer! the crowded excursion for me! the torch-light procession!

The dense brigade, bound for the war, with high piled military wagons following;

People, endless, streaming, with strong voices, passions, pageants;

Manhattan streets, with their powerful throbs, with the beating drums, as now; The endless and noisy chorus, the rustle and clank of muskets, (even the sight of the wounded;)

Manhattan crowds with their turbulent musical chorus—with varied chorus and light of the sparkling eyes;

Manhattan faces and eyes forever for me.

Song of Myself

(FIRST EXCERPT)

I celebrate myself,
And what I assume you shall assume,
For every atom belonging to me as good belongs to you.

I loafe and invite my soul,
I lean and loafe at my ease . . . . observing a spear of summer grass.

Loafe: laze about

(SECOND EXCERPT)

Have you reckoned a thousand acres much? Have you reckoned the earth much?
Have you practiced so long to learn to read?
Have you felt so proud to get at the meaning of poems?

Stop this day and night with me and you shall possess the origin of all poems,
You shall possess the good of the earth and sun . . . . there are millions of suns left,
You shall no longer take things at second or third hand . . . . nor look through the eyes of the
    dead . . . . nor feed on the spectres in books,
You shall not look through my eyes either, nor take things from me,
You shall listen to all sides and filter them from yourself.

Reckoned: considered
Spectres: imagined apparitions

(THIRD EXCERPT)

Walt Whitman, a kosmos, of Manhattan the son,
Turbulent, fleshy, sensual, eating, drinking and breeding,
No sentimentalist, no stander above men and women or apart from them,
No more modest than immodest.

Unscrew the locks from the doors!
Unscrew the doors themselves from their jambs!

Kosmos: universe
Turbulent: not organized or orderly
Sentimentalist: someone who is more
  emotional than sensible

I am of old and young, of the foolish as much as the wise,
Regardless of others, ever regardful of others,
Maternal as well as paternal, a child as well as a man,
Stuffed with the stuff that is coarse, and stuffed with the stuff that is fine,
One of the great nation, the nation of many nations—the smallest the same and the largest the same,
A southerner soon as a northerner, a planter nonchalant and hospitable,
A Yankee bound my own way .... ready for trade .... my joints the limberest joints on earth
      and the sternest joints on earth,
A Kentuckian walking the vale of the Elkhorn in my deerskin leggings,
A boatman over the lakes or bays or along coasts .... a Hoosier, a Badger, a Buckeye,
A Louisianian or Georgian, a poke-easy from sandhills and pines,
At home on Canadian snowshoes or up in the bush, or with fishermen off Newfoundland,
At home in the fleet of iceboats, sailing with the rest and tacking,

At home on the hills of Vermont or in the woods of Maine or the Texan ranch,
Comrade of Californians . . . . comrade of free northwesterners, loving their big proportions,
Comrade of raftsmen and coalmen—comrade of all who shake hands and welcome to drink and meat;
A learner with the simplest, a teacher of the thoughtfulest,
A novice beginning experient of myriads of seasons,
Of every hue and trade and rank, of every caste and religion,
Not merely of the New World but of Africa Europe or Asia . . . . a wandering savage,
A farmer, mechanic, or artist . . . . a gentleman, sailor, lover or quaker,
A prisoner, fancy-man, rowdy, lawyer, physician or priest.

Nonchalant: relaxed
Sternest: firmest
Hoosier: person from Indiana
Badger: someone from Ohio
Poke-easy: easygoing person
Tacking: changing course
Beginning experient: starting to experience
Myriads: countless
Quaker: member of a Christian movement believing in a direct relationship with God
Fancy-man: a man who places particular importance on his appearance

Agonies are one of my changes of garments;
I do not ask the wounded person how he feels . . . . I myself become the wounded person,
My hurt turns livid upon me as I lean on a cane and observe.

I am the mashed fireman with breastbone broken . . . . tumbling walls buried me in their debris,
Heat and smoke I inspired . . . . I heard the yelling shouts of my comrades,
I heard the distant click of their picks and shovels;
They have cleared the beams away . . . . they tenderly lift me forth.

I lie in the night air in my red shirt . . . . the pervading hush is for my sake,
Painless after all I lie, exhausted but not so unhappy,
White and beautiful are the faces around me . . . . the heads are bared of their fire-caps,
The kneeling crowd fades with the light of the torches.

Livid: furiously
Debris: scattered fragments
Pervading: spreading

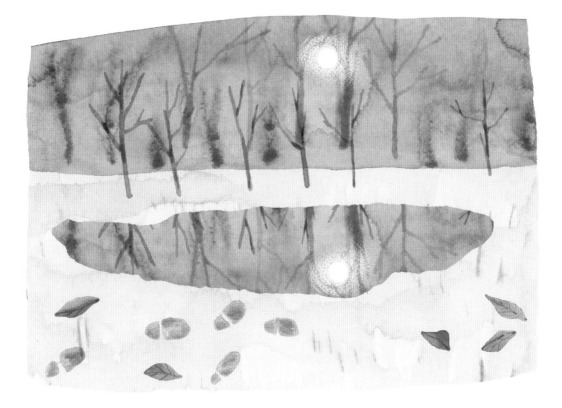

(SIXTH EXCERPT)

I depart as air . . . . I shake my white locks at the runaway sun,
I effuse my flesh in eddies and drift it in lacy jags.
I bequeath myself to the dirt to grow from the grass I love,
If you want me again look for me under your bootsoles.

You will hardly know who I am or what I mean,
But I shall be good health to you nevertheless,
And filter and fibre your blood.

Failing to fetch me at first keep encouraged,
Missing me one place search another,
I stop some where waiting for you

Effuse: to pour forth
Lacy jags: foamy ripples of water
Bequeath: leave or entrust to
Fibre: Walt's version of "fiber;" to add
  substance or to thicken

Shut Not Your Doors

Shut not your doors to me proud libraries,
For that which was lacking on all your well-fill'd shelves, yet needed most, I bring,
Forth from the war emerging, a book I have made,
The words of my book nothing, the drift of it every thing,
A book separate, not link'd with the rest nor felt by the intellect,
But you ye untold latencies will thrill to every page.

Drift: Walt's word for essence or gist, as
  in the saying "get my drift?"
Latencies: hidden things

Calamus 9

Hours continuing long, sore and heavy-hearted,

Hours of the dusk, when I withdraw to a lonesome and unfrequented spot, seating myself, leaning my face in my hands;

Hours sleepless, deep in the night, when I go forth, speeding swiftly the country roads, or through the city streets, or pacing miles and miles, stifling plaintive cries;

Hours discouraged, distracted—for the one I cannot content myself without, soon I saw him content himself without me;

Hours when I am forgotten, (O weeks and months are passing, but I believe I am never to forget!)

Sullen and suffering hours! (I am ashamed—but it is useless—I am what I am;)

Hours of my torment—I wonder if other men ever have the like, out of the like feelings?

Is there even one other like me—distracted—his friend, his lover, lost to him?

Is he too as I am now? Does he still rise in the morning, dejected, thinking who is lost to him? and at night, awaking, think who is lost?

Does he too harbor his friendship silent and endless? harbor his anguish and passion?

Does some stray reminder, or the casual mention of a name, bring the fit back upon him, taciturn and deprest?

Does he see himself reflected in me? In these hours, does he see the face of his hours reflected?

Stifling: holding back
Plaintive: mournful
Taciturn: uncommunicative
Deprest: Walt's version of "depressed"

The Wound-Dresser

Beat! Beat! Drums!

1

Beat! beat! drums!—Blow! bugles! blow!

Through the windows—through doors—burst like a force of ruthless men,

Into the solemn church, and scatter the congregation;

Into the school where the scholar is studying:

Leave not the bridegroom quiet—no happiness must he have now with his bride;

Nor the peaceful farmer any peace, plowing his field or gathering his grain;

So fierce you whirr and pound, you drums—so shrill you bugles blow.

2

Beat! beat! drums!—Blow! bugles! blow!

Over the traffic of cities—over the rumble of wheels in the streets:

Are beds prepared for sleepers at night in the houses?

No sleepers must sleep in those beds;

No bargainers' bargains by day—no brokers or speculators —Would they continue?

Would the talkers be talking? would the singer attempt to sing?

Would the lawyer rise in the court to state his case before the judge?

Then rattle quicker, heavier drums—you bugles wilder blow.

3

Beat! beat! drums!—Blow! bugles! blow!

Make no parley—stop for no expostulation;

Mind not the timid—mind not the weeper or prayer;

Mind not the old man beseeching the young man;

Let not the child's voice be heard, nor the mother's entreaties;

Make even the trestles to shake the dead, where they lie awaiting the hearses,

So strong you thump, O terrible drums—so loud you bugles blow.

*Brokers or speculators: onlookers who do not actively engage in the scene,
  but make money from making bets or taking sides*
Parley: negotiation
Expostulation: protest
Trestles: supporting beams
Hearses: vehicles carrying coffins at funerals

The Wound-Dresser (excerpt)

I dress a wound in the side, deep, deep,
But a day or two more, for see the frame all wasted and sinking,
And the yellow-blue countenance see.

I dress the perforated shoulder, the foot with the bullet-wound,
Cleanse the one with a gnawing and putrid gangrene, so sickening, so offensive,
While the attendant stands behind aside me holding the tray and pail.

I am faithful, I do not give out,
The fractur'd thigh, the knee, the wound in the abdomen,
These and more I dress with impassive hand, (yet deep in my
    breast a fire, a burning flame.)

Frame: body
Countenance: a person's face
Perforated: pierced
Gangrene: decomposition of body tissue because of infection or blocked blood flow
Impassive: not showing emotion

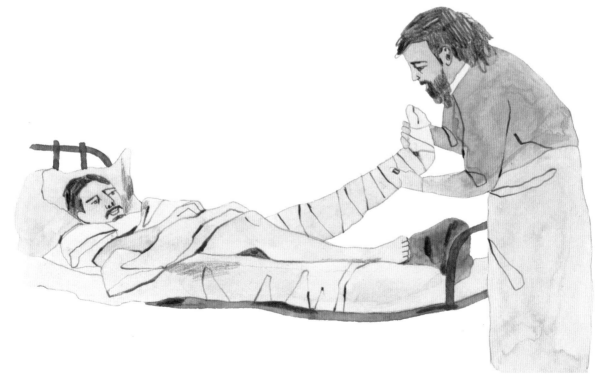

33

Come Up From the Fields Father

Come up from the fields, father, here's a letter from our Pete;
And come to the front door, mother—here's a letter from thy dear son.

Lo, 'tis autumn;
Lo, where the trees, deeper green, yellower and redder,
Cool and sweeten Ohio's villages, with leaves fluttering in the moderate wind;
Where apples ripe in the orchards hang, and grapes on the trellis'd vines;
(Smell you the smell of the grapes on the vines?
Smell you the buckwheat, where the bees were lately buzzing?)

Above all, lo, the sky, so calm, so transparent after the rain, and with wondrous clouds;
Below, too, all calm, all vital and beautiful—and the farm prospers well.

Down in the fields all prospers well;
But now from the fields come, father—come at the daughter's call;
And come to the entry, mother—to the front door come, right away.

Fast as she can she hurries—something ominous— her steps trembling;
She does not tarry to smooth her white hair, nor adjust her cap.

Open the envelope quickly;
O this is not our son's writing, yet his name is sign'd;
O a strange hand writes for our dear son—O stricken mother's soul!
All swims before her eyes—flashes with black—she catches the main words only;
Sentences broken—*gun-shot wound in the breast, cavalry skirmish, taken to hospital,*
At present low, but will soon be better.

Ah, now the single figure to me,
Amid all teeming and wealthy Ohio, with all its cities and farms,
Sickly white in the face and dull in the head, very faint,

By the jamb of a door leans.

Grieve not so, dear mother, (the just-grown daughter speaks through her sobs;
The little sisters huddle around, speechless and dismay'd;)
See, dearest mother, the letter says Pete will soon be better.

Alas, poor boy, he will never be better, (nor may-be needs to be better, that brave and simple soul;)
While they stand at home at the door, he is dead already;
The only son is dead.

But the mother needs to be better;
She, with thin form, presently drest in black;
By day her meals untouch'd—then at night fitfully sleeping, often waking,
In the midnight waking, weeping, longing with one deep longing,
O that she might withdraw unnoticed—silent from life, escape and withdraw,
To follow, to seek, to be with her dear dead son.

Tarry: delay
Teeming: bustling, busy
Dismay'd: distressed

As Toilsome I Wander'd Virginia's Woods

As toilsome I wander'd Virginia's woods,
To the music of rustling leaves kick'd by my feet, (for 'twas autumn,)
   I mark'd at the foot of a tree the grave of a soldier;
Mortally wounded he and buried on the retreat, (easily all could I understand,)
The halt of a mid-day hour, when up! no time to lose—yet this sign left,
On a tablet scrawl'd and nail'd on the tree by the grave,
Bold, cautious, true, and my loving comrade.

Long, long I muse, then on my way go wandering,
Many a changeful season to follow, and many a scene of life,
Yet at times through changeful season and scene, abrupt, alone,
   or in the crowded street,
Comes before me the unknown soldier's grave, comes the inscrip-
   tion rude in Virginia's woods,
Bold, cautious, true, and my loving comrade.

Toilsome: wearily
Mark'd: Walt's version of "marked," or "noted"

36

O Captain! My Captain!

O Captain! my Captain! our fearful trip is done,
The ship has weather'd every rack, the prize we sought is won,
The port is near, the bells I hear, the people all exulting,
While follow eyes the steady keel, the vessel grim and daring;
   But O heart! heart! heart!
    O the bleeding drops of red,
     Where on the deck my Captain lies,
      Fallen cold and dead.

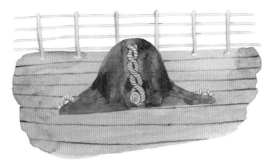

O Captain! my Captain! rise up and hear the bells;
Rise up—for you the flag is flung—for you the bugle trills,
For you bouquets and ribbon'd wreaths—for you the shores
    a-crowding,
For you they call, the swaying mass, their eager faces turning;
   Here Captain! dear father!
    This arm beneath your head!
     It is some dream that on the deck,
      You've fallen cold and dead.

My Captain does not answer, his lips are pale and still,
My father does not feel my arm, he has no pulse nor will,
The ship is anchor'd safe and sound, its voyage closed and
    done,
From fearful trip the victor ship comes in with object won;
   Exult O shores, and ring O bells!
    But I with mournful tread,
     Walk the deck my Captain lies,
      Fallen cold and dead.

Rack: hard blow
Exulting: rejoicing
Keel: a lengthwise structure along the
  bottom of a boat that provides stability
Tread: steps

37

Aboard at a Ship's Helm

Aboard, at the ship's helm,
A young steersman, steering with care.

A bell through fog on a sea-coast dolefully ringing,
An ocean-bell—O a warning bell, rock'd by the waves.

O you give good notice indeed, you bell by the sea-reefs ringing,
Ringing, ringing, to warn the ship from its wreck-place.

For, as on the alert, O steersman, you mind the bell's admonition,
The bows turn,—the freighted ship, tacking, speeds away under her
    gray sails,
The beautiful and noble ship, with all her precious wealth, speeds
    away gaily and safe.

But O the ship, the immortal ship! O ship aboard the ship!
O ship of the body—ship of the soul—voyaging, voyaging, voyaging.

Helm: steering gear of a ship
Dolefully: gloomily

The Good Gray Poet

O Me! O Life!

O me! O life! of the questions of these recurring,

Of the endless trains of the faithless, of cities fill'd with the foolish,

Of myself forever reproaching myself, (for who more foolish than I, and who more faithless?)

Of eyes that vainly crave the light, of the objects mean, of the struggle ever renew'd,

Of the poor results of all, of the plodding and sordid crowds I see around me,

Of the empty and useless years of the rest, with the rest me intertwined,

The question, O me! so sad, recurring—What good amid these, O me, O life?

Answer.

That you are here—that life exists and identity,

That the powerful play goes on, and you may contribute a verse.

Plodding: slow-moving, unexciting
Sordid: dishonorable

On the Beach at Night

On the beach at night,
Stands a child with her father,
Watching the east, the autumn sky.

Up through the darkness,
While ravening clouds, the burial clouds, in black masses spreading,
Lower sullen and fast athwart and down the sky,
Amid a transparent clear belt of ether yet left in the east,
Ascends large and calm the lord-star Jupiter,
And nigh at hand, only a very little above,
Swim the delicate sisters the Pleiades.

From the beach the child holding the hand of her father,
Those burial-clouds that lower victorious soon to devour all,
Watching, silently weeps.

Weep not, child,
Weep not, my darling,
With these kisses let me remove your tears,
The ravening clouds shall not long be victorious,

They shall not long possess the sky, they devour the stars only in apparition,
Jupiter shall emerge, be patient, watch again another night, the Pleiades shall emerge,
They are immortal, all those stars both silvery and golden shall shine out again,
The great stars and the little ones shall shine out again, they endure,
The vast immortal suns and the long-enduring pensive moons shall again shine.

Then dearest child mournest thou only for Jupiter?
Considerest thou alone the burial of the stars?

Something there is,
(With my lips soothing thee, adding I whisper,
I give thee the first suggestion, the problem and indirection,)
Something there is more immortal even than the stars,
(Many the burials, many the days and nights, passing away,)
Something that shall endure longer even than lustrous Jupiter,
Longer than sun or any revolving satellite,
Or the radiant sisters the Pleiades.

Athwart: across
Ether: clear sky; upper regions of air beyond
  the clouds
Nigh: near
Burial-clouds: clouds that cover—and seem
  to bury—the stars
Ravening: very hungry and hunting for prey
Apparition: illusion
Lustrous: radiant
Revolving satellite: a rotating celestial body,
  such as Earth's moon

A Noiseless Patient Spider

A noiseless patient spider,
I mark'd where on a little promontory it stood isolated,
Mark'd how to explore the vacant vast surrounding,
It launch'd forth filament, filament, filament, out of itself,
Ever unreeling them, ever tirelessly speeding them.

And you O my soul where you stand,
Surrounded, detached, in measureless oceans of space,
Ceaselessly musing, venturing, throwing, seeking the spheres to connect them,
Till the bridge you will need be form'd, till the ductile anchor hold,
Till the gossamer thread you fling catch somewhere, O my soul.

Promontory: high point
Vacant: open and free
Filament: a slender thread
Ductile: stretchable yet strong
Gossamer: fine and filmy, as in a thread
 from a cobweb

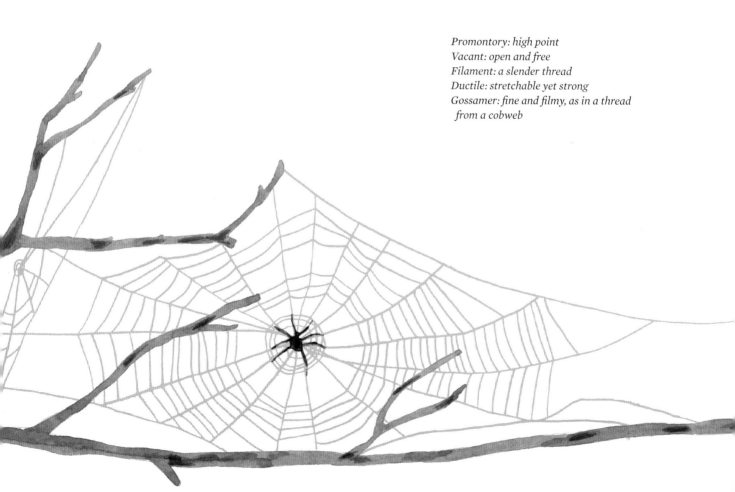

Thanks in Old Age

Thanks in old age—thanks ere I go,
For health, the midday sun, the impalpable air—for life, mere life,
For precious ever-lingering memories, (of you my mother dear—you, father—you, brothers,
    sisters, friends,)
For all my days—not those of peace alone—the days of war the same,
For gentle words, caresses, gifts from foreign lands,
For shelter, wine and meat—for sweet appreciation,
(You distant, dim unknown—or young or old—countless, unspecified, readers belov'd,
We never met, and ne'er shall meet—and yet our souls embrace, long, close and long;)
For beings, groups, love, deeds, words, books—for colors, forms,
For all the brave strong men—devoted, hardy men—who've forward sprung in freedom's help,
    all years, all lands,
For braver, stronger, more devoted men—(a special laurel ere I go, to life's war's chosen ones,
The cannoneers of song and thought—the great artillerists—the foremost leaders, captains of the
    soul:)
As soldier from an ended war return'd—As traveler out of myriads, to the long procession
    retrospective,
Thanks—joyful thanks!—a soldier's, traveler's thanks.

Ere: before
Impalpable: not easily understood or felt
Laurel: honor
Cannoneers: here, Walt means "soldiers" in the
  "war" known as life
Artillerists: more "service people" of "life's war"
Myriads: countless numbers
Procession retrospective: a 'parade of the past.'
  Nearing the end of his life's travels, Walt is
  envisioning his past experiences marching
  before him.

Poets to Come

Poets to come! orators, singers, musicians to come!
Not to-day is to justify me and answer what I am for,
But you, a new brood, native, athletic, continental, greater than before known,
Arouse! for you must justify me.

I myself but write one or two indicative words for the future,
I but advance a moment only to wheel and hurry back in the darkness.

I am a man who, sauntering along without fully stopping, turns a casual look upon you and then
   averts his face,
Leaving it to you to prove and define it,
Expecting the main things from you.

Continental: characteristic of a continent; here, Walt means "expansive"
Indicative: representative
Sauntering: strolling

What Walt Was Thinking

***Song of the Open Road* (1892):** Here, at the start of our journey through Whitman's life and work, Walt urges you to join him on the open road. He asks you to leave behind your papers, books, and doubts, and instead take his hand and experience the adventure of your lifetime.

***There Was a Child Went Forth* (1855):** Walt believed experiences form our characters, from our earliest interactions with the world to what we're doing right now. Here, he explores this idea in which he recalls seemingly unimportant memories of his childhood on a Long Island farm — experiences that helped to make him the poet he became.

***Paumanok* (1892):** Published near the end of his life, this poem demonstrates Walt's enduring affection for his birthplace: Long Island. He preferred to call it "Paumanok" as a tribute to the island's Native American roots. His love of sea imagery in his poems is rooted in his early years exploring Long Island's beaches.

***The Sleepers* (1855):** The poet here recalls a tale of his mother's aborted friendship with a local squaw. Long Island's indigenous population would be nearly obliterated during Walt's own lifetime, and his mother's personal loss in the story echoes the new country's disconnection from its aboriginal roots.

***Out of the Cradle Endlessly Rocking* (1860):** In the first excerpt, Walt claims that his poetic gift was not given to him by teachers or even his family, but by nature. In the second excerpt, the boy is overcome with joy when he realizes that he can understand the birds — and then devastated to learn that one of them never returns to his mate. He then listens to the tragic song of the he-bird ... and realizes that he has discovered his own poetic voice.

***Beginning My Studies* (1892):** As a teacher in his late teens and early 20s, Whitman used what were considered progressive techniques — such as encouraging students to discuss rather than simply memorize and recite and inventing educational games. In this poem, we meet one of his ideal pupils: someone who might not like lessons or lectures, but obviously loves to learn.

***When I Heard the Learn'd Astronomer* (1865):** Walt went to Brooklyn's first public school but wasn't the type to benefit from a traditional education. This poem hints at why: Walt would rather look at the universe with the naked eye rather than the most sophisticated calibrated telescope. Science is a noble pursuit that is necessary to sustain and better our lives; poetry is what we stay alive for.

***Crossing Brooklyn Ferry* (1892):** When Walt was four years old, his father moved the growing Whitman family from their farm to the bustling city of Brooklyn. Although Walt always cherished a connection with nature, he quickly fell in love with urban life. In this much-loved poem, the narrator connects with us future readers by thinking about how we, too, will be fascinated by this colorful and ever-moving cityscape.

***A Font of Type* (1892):** Walt had to drop out of school at age eleven to help support his seven siblings. First working for a lawyer, he eventually found work in a printing office. It was a lucky accident: Printing is the only working class profession in which being able to read is an important skill. This poem celebrates what to most folks looks like an ordinary typewritten page, but to Walt is a gorgeous sea of possibility.

Walt Whitman's Caution **(1860):** By age 27, Walt had worked his way up to the position of editor of the *Brooklyn Daily Eagle*, an important newspaper. This helped Walt shape and define his politics, which grew more radical through the 1840s and '50s. He was fired after less than two years for his anti-slavery beliefs. This poem contains a line that might have irritated some of his employers, but has become a favorite of his readers.

I Sing the Body Electric **(1856):** When Walt visited New Orleans in his 28th year, he witnessed his first slave auction in a public square. The experience had a strong effect on his feelings about racism and abolition, as can be seen from this excerpt from a poem first titled "Poem of a Black Person." He "helps" the slave auctioneer by drawing attention to the pricelessness of the slave — who has the same qualities and potential as the rest of humankind, including the auctioneer himself.

A Woman Waits for Me **(1860):** Women's rights and abolitionism were two revolutionary movements that developed simultaneously in the mid-nineteenth century. In his journalism, Walt had long defended women's rights for fair salaries and equal treatment. This poem celebrates their strength of character as well as their physical bodies. His ideas were considered so progressive that this poem was banned from publication in 1882.

City of Ships **(1865):** Manhattan was a microcosm of the world to Walt. Its energy and spectacular show of progress and ambition inspired him to his own form of greatness.

Give Me the Splendid Silent Sun **(1865):** Walt's trip to the Midwest and the South in 1848 gave him his first experience of the rest of America beyond New York. In the first part of the poem, Walt celebrates the people, scenes, and more relaxed lifestyle that he encountered while on the road. In the second part, Walt takes back everything he just said and bares his city soul. He fell in love with New York at a time when other writers simply did not find inspiration or even a reason to live in the city. Walt felt energized instead of overwhelmed by its constant motion, heard music instead of madness in its street din, and saw humanity instead of strangeness in its crowds.

Song of Myself, first excerpt **(1855):** From the very first lines of the first poem in *Leaves of Grass*, we readers are invited to a new way of thinking — about the purpose of poetry, our relationship with our poets, and the "United" idea of the States. We start by reconsidering the grass that we often simply stroll over. As the most democratic of plants, grass represents America: Each leaf is important to the idea of the whole.

Song of Myself, second excerpt **(1855):** Walt conceived of *Leaves of Grass* as America's cultural Declaration of Independence. This document, like the original written by the Founding Fathers, promises a new beginning, new freedoms ... a New World.

Song of Myself, third excerpt **(1892):** The collection of poems entitled *Leaves of Grass* was the product of a fiercely independent spirit. No publisher was willing to risk his reputation on twelve radical poems written by a relative nobody, so Walt designed the book himself, printing and publishing it with the help of Brooklyn friends and neighbors.

Song of Myself, fourth excerpt **(1855):** Walt hoped to provide a vivid, sweeping image of America in such catalogs as this one. Can you find yourself in it?

Song of Myself, fifth excerpt **(1855):** As a journalist, Whitman "became" his subjects in order to better understand and connect with them. These lines are surely inspired by his reporting of New York's great fires in the 1840s.

Song of Myself, sixth excerpt **(1855):** Walt's struggle to keep the conversation going with us readers is evident near the end of "Song of Myself," the longest and best-known poem in *Leaves of Grass*. He makes it clear that he is present — in the air, in our water, in the ground beneath our feet. Besides the meaning of his words, the typesetting of these famous last lines, particularly the missing final period, suggest that he is indeed waiting somewhere for us.

Shut Not Your Doors (1892): Walt never achieved the success he imagined for his poetic experiment, *Leaves of Grass*. Here, he defies the many critics of his unusual writing style and subjects, and dares readers to appreciate his book's individuality and innovations.

Calamus 9 (1860): While America's struggle with the issue of slavery resulted in a major political crisis, Whitman's desire to love and be loved brought about his own profound emotional crisis. Perhaps his most personal poem is "Calamus 9," in which the poet asks difficult questions about his identity and wonders if anyone else is suffering because of similar feelings and doubts. The poem ends with questions that reach out to us. Many have found in this poem the brave voice of a person who tried to express himself freely — not just who he was, but whom he chose to love.

Beat! Beat! Drums! (1865): On April 12, 1861, Whitman read about the first shots fired at Fort Sumter, South Carolina. The Civil War had begun. This popular poem conveys Whitman's initial excitement about the prospect of fighting in the name of justice, equality, and union.

The Wound-Dresser (1892): Too old to take part in the fighting, Walt volunteered in the makeshift hospital tents that were scattered around Washington D.C., and thus was a firsthand witness to the war's aftermath. "The Wound-Dresser" provides graphic images of what Whitman must have seen in over two years of service to the solders. It also hints at his suppressed anger regarding the terrible casualties of the Civil War.

Come Up From the Fields Father (1865): From early 1863 to the end of the Civil War in the spring of 1865, Walt visited army hospitals daily and wrote hundreds of letters that briefed families on soldiers' conditions. It was his way of connecting Americans during a war that threatened to tear the country apart. In this poem, Whitman the letter writer is a "silent" witness to one family tragedy, which represents so many others.

As Toilsome I Wander'd Virginia's Woods (1892): Part of Walt's mission as a poet was to make sure his country never forgot the great sacrifice it had made to achieve union. Many of his greatest poems of the Civil War seek to humanize the daunting numbers of the dead and to remind Americans that each of these victims deserves commemoration and respect.

O Captain! My Captain! (1892): On April 14, 1865, five days after the April 9th surrender of Confederate commanding general Robert E. Lee, President Abraham Lincoln was assassinated. Whitman had felt a special bond with Lincoln because of their shared humble roots and their position on slavery and abolition. The loss of the "Captain" of the Union's "ship" was thus also a personal one for Whitman, who describes Lincoln as "father." The poem isn't written in his typical style — note its regular rhyme and rhythm, and its use of a subject that is not Whitman, for a change — and yet it is one of his most popular works.

Aboard at a Ship's Helm (1867): Though the Union Army had won the war, Lincoln's assassination left the country's fate in doubt. Walt's poetry right after the war reflects these insecurities. Soon after composing "O Captain! My Captain!", Walt picked up on the ship imagery once again, this time placing a new and inexperienced captain at the helm.

O Me! O Life! (1892): The years leading up to the Civil War as well as the war itself were troubled times for Walt. The speaker of this poem asks a question about existence that expresses his frustration — and then courageously answers it, reminding us that we all have a role in the ongoing drama of life. What will your verse be?

On the Beach at Night (1867): Whitman's postwar questions and worries led to the composition of poems focused on the concept of immortality. Looking at the stars and planets while standing on the shore with her father, a young girl worries that they have disappeared forever behind the clouds. Her father comforts her by telling her that they will re-emerge and endure. She (and we) are left wondering: Is there really such a thing as death?

A Noiseless Patient Spider (1892): In this favorite poem, a tiny insect represents the depths of a human soul. This late composition also shows that Walt — who had built his career on being the poet of the "now" — was setting his sights on the future, as the spider cast his line into unknown space.

Thanks in Old Age (1892): Whitman had much to be thankful for by the time he died at age 72 on March 26, 1892. He had grown his *Leaves* through six different editions and from twelve to over 400 poems. He had served his country during the Civil War. He had many enduring friendships and had even had a great love in his life. Most importantly, he had been true to himself and his poetic vision. He never compromised and always followed his heart. In this poem, Whitman expresses gratitude for life's everyday joys.

Poets to Come (1892): The poets to come ... are us! Walt reaches out beyond the confines of time and asks us to carry his message into the future. He has supplied the canvas and a few words of guidance, but we are to paint the masterpiece.

Index

"A Font of Type," 16

"A Noiseless Patient Spider," 42

"A Woman Waits for Me" (excerpt), 20

"Aboard at a Ship's Helm," 38

"As Toilsome I Wander'd Virginia's Woods," 36

"Beat! Beat! Drums!," 32

"Beginning My Studies," 13

"Calamus 9," 31

"City of Ships" (excerpt), 21

"Come Up From the Fields Father," 34

"Crossing Brooklyn Ferry" (three excerpts), 14

"Give Me the Splendid Silent Sun," 22

"I Sing the Body Electric" (excerpt), 18

"O Captain! My Captain!," 37

"O Me! O Life!," 39

"On the Beach at Night," 40

"Out of the Cradle Endlessly Rocking" (two excerpts), 12

"Paumanok," 10

"Poets to Come," 44

"Shut Not Your Doors," 30

"Song of Myself" (six excerpts), 24

"Song of the Open Road" (excerpt), 7

"Thanks in Old Age," 43

"The Sleepers" (excerpt), 11

"The Wound-Dresser" (excerpt), 33

"There Was a Child Went Forth" (two excerpts), 8

"Walt Whitman's Caution," 17

"When I Heard the Learn'd Astronomer," 13